Self-Publishing Mastery Toolkit

© 2025 KASA Online.Africa

All rights reserved. No part of this publication may be reproduced, stored in a retrieval system, or transmitted in any form or by any means—electronic, mechanical, photocopying, recording, or otherwise—without prior written permission of the publisher, except in the case of brief quotations used in reviews or articles.

Published by:

KASA Online.Africa

ISBN: 978-1-0492-0889-3

First Edition – 2025

Disclaimer:

This book is designed to provide accurate and authoritative information on the subject matter covered. It is sold with the understanding that the publisher is not engaged in rendering legal, financial, or professional advice. If expert assistance is required, the services of a competent professional should be sought.

Cover Design: Qhubokuhle Mduduzi Ntuli

Interior Design & Layout: KASA Online.Africa

Dedication

This book is dedicated to all authors around the world—to every dreamer who has ever held a story in their heart and longed to share it with the world.

To the bold and vibrant voices of Africa, and to the resilient storytellers of South Africa, who continue to shape narratives that carry our history, our struggles, and our hopes into the future.

And especially to those who are just stepping into the publishing space—new authors taking their very first flight. Just as a pilot treasures a manual for guidance in the skies, may this book be your reliable companion, a steady hand as you navigate the world of self-publishing.

This book is your ever-present friend, designed to help you take your manuscript from idea to bestseller. It is written for you, to support your journey, to cheer for your victories, and to guide you through the challenges.

May your words inspire generations.

May your stories echo beyond borders.

May your journey as an author be filled with courage, joy, and limitless creativity.

This book is dedicated to you.

Preface / Introduction

Every book begins as a spark—an idea, a memory, or a story that refuses to stay silent. For many aspiring authors, that spark burns brightly, but somewhere between inspiration and publication, the path becomes unclear. Too often, manuscripts gather dust, not because they lack brilliance, but because their authors lack the right tools, guidance, and confidence to bring them to life.

This book was written to change that.

Think of it as your flight manual for self-publishing. Just as pilots rely on proven checklists and structured systems to navigate the skies, so too can writers rely on this guide to navigate the publishing journey. Whether you are penning your very first manuscript or polishing your tenth, this toolkit is designed to keep you steady, informed, and motivated as you take off toward authorship success.

What can you expect from these pages?

- **Clarity** – breaking down complex publishing processes into simple, actionable steps.

- **Confidence** – helping you see that self-publishing is not just possible, but powerful.
- **Practical Tools** – from writing and editing, to formatting, cover design, marketing, and beyond.
- **Global & Local Perspectives** – insights into opportunities worldwide (like Amazon KDP, eBooks, and audiobooks), as well as unique possibilities within Africa and South Africa.

Most importantly, you can expect a **companion**. This is not a book to skim and shelve—it is a book to walk with, refer back to, and lean on at every stage of your journey.

If you have ever doubted your ability to become a published author, let this book quiet those doubts. The world is waiting for your voice, your story, your contribution.

Welcome aboard. Your publishing journey starts here.

Contents

Self-Publishing Mastery Toolkit – Full Course Outline

Target Audience

- **Aspiring writers** (fiction, non-fiction, poetry, children's books, coloring books, memoirs, etc.)
- **Creators** who want to turn their knowledge into books
- **Entrepreneurs** who want to use books as business tools (brand authority, lead generation)

MODULE 1: The Foundations of Writing for Publishing

- Why self-publishing is an opportunity today
- Identifying your book idea (fiction vs. non-fiction)
- Outlining techniques (story arcs, chapter mapping, content frameworks)
- Building a writing routine and avoiding writer's block

Activities/Tools:

- Book idea brainstorming worksheet
- Fiction & non-fiction outline templates
- Writing tracker spreadsheet

MODULE 2: Editing & Proofing Essentials

- Levels of editing (developmental, copy, proofreading)
- DIY editing tips + recommended free/paid software (Grammarly, ProWritingAid, Hemingway)
- How to find & work with freelance editors
- Beta readers & feedback circles

Activities/Tools:

- Self-editing checklist
- Editable sample chapter (before/after editing)
- Beta reader feedback form

MODULE 3: Book Design & Formatting

- Anatomy of a book (front matter, main content, back matter)
- Cover design (DIY tools like Canva vs. hiring a designer)
- Formatting for print (paperback, hardcover)
- Formatting for digital (Kindle, ePub, PDF, interactive books)

Activities/Tools:

- DIY cover template pack
- Formatting guide (Word, Google Docs, or InDesign basics)
- Sample layout files

MODULE 4: Publishing Platforms & Options

- Self-publishing vs. traditional publishing (pros & cons)
- Amazon KDP deep dive (setup, royalties, categories, keywords)
- Other platforms: IngramSpark, Lulu, Draft2Digital, Smashwords, Kobo
- ISBN, barcodes, and copyright basics

Activities/Tools:

- Step-by-step KDP account setup guide
- ISBN application guide (local + international)
- Royalty comparison chart

MODULE 5: Marketing & Branding for Authors

- Building an author brand & online presence
- Social media strategies for writers
- Email list building for authors
- Pre-launch, launch, and post-launch strategies
- How to get reviews & book bloggers interested

Activities/Tools:

- Author brand worksheet
- Launch day checklist
- Email sequence templates for book release

MODULE 6: Monetization Beyond the Book

How to turn a book into:

- A course
- A podcast
- An audiobook
- Paid workshops/webinars
- Licensing, translations, and global distribution
- Creating merchandise from your book (planners, coloring books, quotes)

Activities/Tools:

- Repurposing roadmap (book → course → product)
- Audiobook checklist
- Merch design starter kit

BONUS MODULE: Self-Publishing in South Africa (or Adaptable by Region)

- Local ISBN process (National Library of South Africa)
- SA distribution options (Takealot, bookstores, local print-on-demand)
- Payment & tax considerations for South African authors

Final Course Extras

- Lifetime access with updates (since platforms change)
- Completion certificate
- Downloadable manual (all lessons combined into a single ebook/PDF)
- Option for private coaching upsell

MODULE 1: FOUNDATIONS OF WRITING FOR PUBLISHING

Learning Outcomes

By the end of this module, learners will be able to:

- Identify a strong book idea suitable for publishing.
- Outline their book in a structured way.
- Build a consistent writing routine.
- Overcome writer's block and stay motivated.

Lesson 1: Why Self-Publishing Is an Opportunity Today

Traditional publishing vs. self-publishing

1. **Traditional = slow, selective, limited royalties.**
    1.1 **Traditional Publishing: The Old Standard:**
    - Traditional publishing has long been the "official" route to becoming an author. But it comes with limitations.
    - Slow – Publishing can take 1–2 years from acceptance to bookstore shelves.
    - Selective – Only a small percentage of manuscripts are chosen. Rejection rates are extremely high.
    - Limited Royalties – Authors often earn just 5–15% of the cover price, while publishers, distributors, and bookstores take the majority.
    - Control Sacrificed – Publishers may change titles, covers, or even storylines to fit their business model.

Takeaway: Traditional publishing offers prestige but limits authors' earnings, control, and speed to market.

2. **Self-publishing = fast, accessible, higher royalties.**
    2.1 Self-Publishing: The Author as Entrepreneur

- Self-publishing empowers writers to take control of their own journey. With platforms like Amazon KDP, Draft2Digital, IngramSpark, and local printing solutions, anyone can become both the writer and publisher.
- Fast – Books can be published in weeks, not years.
- Accessible – No gatekeepers. Anyone can publish worldwide.
- Higher Royalties – On Amazon KDP, royalties can reach 35–70%—far higher than traditional deals.
- Creative Freedom – Authors choose their own title, cover, design, and marketing strategy.

Takeaway: Self-publishing offers speed, control, and higher financial rewards—but requires personal effort in editing, design, and promotion.

3. Global book market growth (Amazon KDP, eBooks, audiobooks).

3.1 Global Book Market Growth

- The publishing world is expanding beyond traditional print.
- Amazon KDP has become the world's largest self-publishing platform, giving authors instant global reach.
- EBooks continue to grow in popularity due to affordability and convenience.
- Audiobooks are the fastest-growing format, powered by platforms like Audible and Google Play Books.
- Indie Authors are increasingly becoming bestsellers, proving that self-publishing is not "second class" but a real business model.

Takeaway: The global publishing market is more open than ever—self-publishing is not just possible, it's profitable.

4. Local opportunities (niche audiences, self-publishing in South Africa and other regions).

4.1 Local & Regional Opportunities (South Africa and Beyond)

- For South African and African authors, self-publishing is more than just a business—it's an opportunity to **tell stories** that are often overlooked by mainstream publishers.
- **Niche Audiences** – Books in African languages and culturally unique stories have a growing market but limited supply.
- **Direct Sales** – Authors can sell through schools, churches, events, and community book fairs.

- **Local Online Stores** – Platforms like Takealot, Loot, Exclusive Books Online offer space for indie authors.
- **Payment Gateways** – Tools like PayFast, PayGate, Yoco make it easy for authors to sell ebooks and audiobooks directly.

Takeaway: In regions like South Africa, self-publishing is a powerful tool for cultural preservation, empowerment, and reaching underserved readers.

Key Insight for Learners

Self-publishing is not just an alternative to traditional publishing—it's a modern opportunity to **own your work, reach global and local audiences, and earn higher royalties while telling the stories that matter to you and your community.**

Activity:

Compare Your Publishing Paths

- This activity helps you reflect on the differences between **traditional publishing** and **self-publishing** and decide which might fit your goals.
- Reflection prompt: **"Why do I want to publish a book?** What **impact** do I want it to have?"

Step 1: Quick Comparison Chart

Aspect	Traditional Publishing	Self-Publishing
Speed to market		
Who makes decisions		
Royalties & earnings		
Control over creativity		
Distribution reach		

Step 2: Reflection Questions

1. If you published a book today, which route feels more appealing to you, and why?

2. What scares you most about self-publishing?

3. What excites you most about self-publishing?

4. Do you think your book idea would work better in a global market (like Amazon) or a local market (like South Africa)?

Step 3: Takeaway Statement

Write a one-sentence statement below to summarize your current mindset about publishing:

"For my author journey, I think _____ publishing is best because _____."

___

Lesson 2: Identifying Your Audience & Niche

- **Fiction ideas:** inspired by imagination, life experiences, or "What if?" questions.
- **Non-fiction ideas:** based on expertise, life lessons, or solving a problem for readers.
- **Poetry/children's books/coloring books:** creative formats that are always in demand.

1. Why Understanding Your Audience Matters

Knowing your **audience** is essential before writing. It helps you:
- Write content that **resonates** with readers.
- Decide the **tone, style, and language** of your book.
- Identify **marketing channels** to reach your readers.
- Increase **sales and engagement** by targeting the right niche.

Key Insight: A book without a clear audience is harder to sell and less impactful.

2. Defining Your Reader Avatar

A **reader avatar** is a detailed description of your ideal reader. Consider:
- A **reader avatar** is a detailed description of your ideal reader. Consider:
- **Demographics** – Age, gender, location, education, occupation.
- **Interests & Hobbies** – What they like, read, watch, or follow.
- **Challenges & Pain Points** – Problems your book can help solve.
- **Goals & Aspirations** – What they hope to achieve or experience.

Example:

> ➤ *"My ideal reader is a 28-year-old South African entrepreneur who wants to self-publish a motivational business book. She struggles with marketing and needs actionable advice to succeed."*

3. Choosing Your Niche

- Your **niche** is a smaller, specific segment of a larger market.
- Helps your book stand out in a **crowded marketplace.**
- Allows you to **target marketing** more effectively.

Examples:

- **Global market:** EBooks' on personal finance, self-help, or productivity.
- **Local market:** Books in African languages or culturally-relevant topics.
- **Hybrid:** Niche topics with both local and global appeal.

Tip: Research platforms like Amazon, local online bookstores, and social media groups to see what readers are already seeking.

5. Tools to Research Your Audience

- **Google Trends** – Check interest over time.
- **Social Media Groups & Forums** – See what readers are discussing.
- **Book Reviews** – Read reviews on similar books to understand gaps.
- **Surveys & Questionnaires** – Ask potential readers directly.

Key Insight: The more you know your audience, the easier it is to write a book that sells and impacts lives.

Activity:

Define Your Reader & Niche

This activity helps you create a **reader avatar** and identify your niche before writing.

Step 1: Create Your Reader Avatar

Fill out the table below:

Aspect	Description
Name / Nickname	
Age / Gender	
Location	
Occupation / Education	
Interests & Hobbies	
Challenges / Pain Points	
Goals / Aspirations	

Step 2: Identify Your Niche

Answer the questions:

1. What **specific topic** does your book focus on?

2. Who will benefit **most** from reading it?

3. How does your book **stand out** from others in this topic?

Step 3: Reflection Statement

Write a one-sentence statement summarizing your audience and niche:

"My ideal reader is _____, and my book focuses on _____ because _____."

Lesson 3: Planning Your Book – Structure & Outline

1. Why Planning Matters

A well-structured book ensures your ideas flow logically and keeps readers engaged. Planning helps you:

- Avoid writer's block by having a **clear roadmap.**
- Maintain **consistency** in tone, style, and pacing.
- Save time during writing and editing.
- Ensure your book delivers **value to your audience.**

Key Insight: Successful self-published books often start with a solid outline and plan.

2. Key Components of a Book Outline

2.1 Title & Subtitle
- Captures attention and clearly conveys what the book is about.
- Should reflect the audience and niche you defined in Lesson 2.

2.2 Introduction / Preface
- Explains the purpose of the book and what readers will gain.
- Connects with your audience emotionally

2.3 Chapters / Sections
- Break content into manageable parts.
- Each chapter should focus on a specific idea or lesson.
- Use headings, subheadings, and bullet points for clarity.

2.4 Conclusion / Summary
- Recap main points.
- Encourage readers to take action (especially for self-help, business, or educational books).

2.5 Additional Materials (Optional)
- Worksheets, exercises, charts, or references.
- Useful for books designed to teach or guide readers.

3. Creating a Chapter-by-Chapter Outline

- **Step 1:** List the main ideas you want to cover in your book.

- **Step 2:** Group related ideas into chapters or sections.
- **Step 3:** Add subtopics, examples, and exercises under each chapter.
- **Step 4:** Review the flow – ensure it progresses logically from start to finish.

Tip: For fiction, you can use a plot outline, including characters, conflicts, and story arcs.

4. Tools to Plan Your Book

- **Digital tools:** Scrivener, Notion, Google Docs, Microsoft Word
- **Mind mapping:** XMind, MindMeister, or pen & paper
- **Templates:** Pre-made book outline templates (many free online)
- **Sticky notes or index cards:** For flexible chapter reordering

Activity: Build Your Book Outline

Step 1: Book Overview

Element	Your Plan
Working Title	
Subtitle / Tagline	
Purpose / Goal	
Target Audience	

Step 2: Chapter Planning

Chapter Number	Chapter Title / Topic	Subtopics / Key Points	Notes / Examples
1.			
2.			
3.			
4.			
5.			

Tip: Add more rows as needed.

Step 3: Reflection Statement

"My book is structured to deliver _____ to my readers, and I plan to cover it through _____ chapters focusing on _____."

_____

Lesson 4: Writing Techniques – Style, Tone & Voice

1. **Why Writing Style Matters**
   - Your writing style is how your ideas are expressed. It helps you:
   - Connect with your audience emotionally.
   - Communicate your message clearly.
   - Make your book distinctive and memorable.

Key Insight: Style affects how readers perceive your credibility and how enjoyable your book is to read.

2. **Understanding Tone**
   - **Tone** is the emotional feel of your writing. It should match your audience and purpose.
   - **Formal:** Professional, academic, or business books.
   - **Casual / Conversational:** Self-help, lifestyle, or creative books.
   - **Inspirational / Motivational:** Encouraging, uplifting, and persuasive.

Tip: Read examples from your niche to identify tones that resonate with readers.

3. **Developing Your Voice**
   - Voice is your unique personality expressed through writing.
   - Consistent voice helps readers recognize and trust you.

Techniques to develop voice:

   - Write like you speak (natural rhythm).
   - Use personal stories or examples.
   - Maintain consistency in word choice, sentence structure, and perspective.

Example: J.K. Rowling's voice is imaginative and descriptive, while Malcolm Gladwell's voice is analytical and engaging.

4. **Practical Writing Techniques**
   - **Show, Don't Tell** – Use examples, stories, or analogies.
   - **Vary Sentence Length** – Keep readers engaged with rhythm.
   - **Active Voice** – "The cat chased the mouse" is stronger than "The mouse was chased by the cat."
   - **Clarity & Simplicity** – Avoid jargon unless your audience expects it.
   - **Editing & Revising** – First drafts are rarely perfect. Editing improves clarity, flow, and readability.

Activity: Analyze & Apply Your Writing Style

Step 1: Identify Tone & Voice

Choose your book's tone and describe it:

Aspect	Description
Tone	
Voice	

Step 2: Write a Sample Paragraph

- Use your chosen tone and voice.
- Focus on clarity, engagement, and flow.

  ➢ *"Write 3–5 sentences introducing your book or topic in your voice and tone."*

Step 3: Reflection Statement

  ➢ *"For my book, I will use a _____ tone and a _____ voice to connect with my audience and make my content engaging because _____."*

Lesson 5: Overcoming Writer's Block

1. **What is Writer's Block?**

Writer's block is a temporary inability to produce new writing or ideas. It's common and can happen to anyone.

Key Insight: Recognizing it early allows you to apply strategies to overcome it quickly.

2. **Common Causes of Writer's Block**
   - **Perfectionism** – Fear that your writing isn't "good enough."
   - **Lack of clarity** – Unclear ideas or purpose.
   - **Distractions** – Digital or environmental interruptions.
   - **Fatigue / Stress** – Mental or physical exhaustion.
   - **Overthinking** – Worrying too much about audience reception.

3. **Strategies to Overcome Writer's Block**
   - **Set Small Goals**: Write for 10–15 minutes at a time.
     Focus on completing a paragraph or section rather than the whole chapter.
   - **Freewriting** : Write continuously without worrying about grammar or structure.
     Helps ideas flow and reduces pressure.
   - **Change Your Environment:**
     Move to a different room, go outside, or rearrange your workspace.
   - **Use Prompts & Exercises:**
     Answer questions, write about your topic from a new angle, or describe an example.
   - **Take Breaks & Relax:**
     Step away from writing to refresh your mind.
     Exercise, meditate, or listen to music to stimulate creativity.
   - **Outline Before Writing:**
     Having a clear structure reduces uncertainty and makes starting easier.

4. **Tools & Techniques**
   - **Digital tools:** Scrivener, Notion, MindMeister (for idea organization)
   - **Timers:** Pomodoro technique to focus in short bursts
   - **Writing communities:** Support and feedback from peers

- **Journaling:** Capture thoughts and ideas daily

Activity: Overcoming Your Writer's Block

Step 1: Identify the Cause

Possible Cause	Is this affecting you? (Yes/No)	Notes / Observations
Perfectionism		
Lack of clarity		
Distractions		
Fatigue / Stress		
Overthinking		

Step 2: Apply Strategies

- Choose 1–3 strategies to overcome your specific cause(s).
- Write down how you will implement them:

Strategy   **How You Will Apply It**

Step 3: Reflection Statement

> "I will overcome my writer's block by _____ because it addresses my challenge of _____, allowing me to continue writing effectively."

End-of-Module Wrap-Up: Reflection & Next Steps

1. Reflect on Your Progress

Take a moment to review everything you've learned in this module. Use the questions below to guide your reflection:

Reflection Question	Your Response
Have you chosen a book idea?	
Do you have a rough outline for your book?	
Do you have a writing plan or schedule?	

> *Tip: Be honest with yourself. Progress isn't about perfection—it's about taking consistent steps forward.*

2. Celebrate Your Achievements

- You have completed the foundation lessons of writing for publishing.
- You understand the difference between traditional and self-publishing.
- You have explored your reader, niche, and book structure.
- You have learned techniques to overcome writer's block.

Encouragement:

> "You are now officially a writer in progress!"

3. Next Steps

- **Refine Your Book Idea**
  Revisit your reader avatar and niche to ensure alignment.
- **Complete Your Book Outline**
  Use your chapter planning and idea organization tables.
- **Set a Writing Schedule**
  Decide how many words or pages to write daily/weekly.
  Include time for research, writing, and editing.
- **Stay Motivated & Consistent**

Track your progress and reward small milestones.

Join writing communities or share updates with accountability partners.

4. Reflection Statement

> *"After completing Module 1, I feel _____ about my writing progress. My book idea is _____, my outline is _____, and my next steps are _____."*

MODULE 2: EDITING & PROOFING ESSENTIALS

Learning Outcomes

By the end of this module, learners will:

- Understand different levels of editing.
- Use tools and techniques for self-editing.
- Learn when and how to work with editors or beta readers.
- Apply proofreading basics to polish their manuscript.

Lesson 1: Levels of Editing

1. Why Editing Matters

Editing transforms a draft into a polished, professional book. It ensures your ideas are clear, coherent, and engaging.

Key Insight: Self-published books that are well-edited gain credibility, retain readers, and increase sales potential.

2. Three Main Levels of Editing

Level of Editing	Purpose	What It Focuses On
Developmental / Structural Editing	Big-picture editing	Plot, chapter flow, structure, clarity, pacing, and content consistency
Line / Stylistic Editing	Sentence-level refinement	Clarity, tone, voice, word choice, sentence variety, repetition
Copyediting / Proofreading	Polishing & correctness	Grammar, punctuation, spelling, formatting, consistency, typos

Tip: Many writers hire professionals for developmental and copyediting stages but can do initial line edits themselves.

3. When to Apply Each Level

- **Developmental / Structural Editing** – After completing the first full draft.
- **Line / Stylistic Editing** – After addressing structural issues; focuses on improving readability.
- **Copyediting / Proofreading** – Final stage before publishing; ensures your manuscript is error-free.

Key Insight: Skipping levels can result in a book that feels unpolished or confusing.

4. Tools & Resources for Editing

- **Software Tools:** Grammarly, ProWritingAid, Hemingway Editor
- **Manual Techniques:** Reading aloud, backward reading (proofreading sentences in reverse), peer feedback
- **Professional Services:** Freelance editors, editing agencies, beta readers

Activity: Assess Your Editing Needs

Take a sample paragraph → identify what changes belong to developmental, line, copy, or proof edits.

Step 1: Evaluate Your Manuscript

Editing Level	Do you need it? (Yes/No)	Notes / Observations
Developmental / Structural		
Line / Stylistic		
Copyediting / Proofreading		

Step 2: Plan Your Editing Process

Stage	Actions	Tools / Resources	Timeline
1			

2			
3			

Step 3: Reflection Statement

"For my manuscript, I will apply _____ editing first because _____. My overall editing plan will ensure my book is _____ for readers."

Lesson 2: Self-Editing Tools & Techniques

1. Why Self-Editing Matters

Even before hiring an editor (or if you can't afford one), self-editing helps you refine your manuscript. It allows you to fix obvious issues, polish your voice, and present a cleaner draft—saving time and money in later editing stages.

2. Key Self-Editing Techniques

Technique	How It Works	Benefits
Read Aloud	Read your text out loud	Helps identify awkward phrasing, run-on sentences, and rhythm issues
Print & Review	Review a printed copy	Spot formatting errors and typos missed on screen
Reverse Reading	Read sentences backwards (end → start)	Forces attention to detail for spelling and punctuation
Cut Unnecessary Words	Remove filler words like very, really, just	Sharpens your writing and improves clarity
Check Consistency	Verify names, places, tense, formatting	Prevents confusion for readers

3. Digital Self-Editing Tools

Tool	Purpose	Best For
Grammarly	Grammar, spelling, readability	Everyday corrections

ProWritingAid	In-depth style, grammar, structure checks	Serious writers needing detailed reports
Hemingway Editor	Simplifies complex sentences	Improving clarity and readability
Google Docs / Word Track Changes	Collaboration and revision tracking	Peer or editor feedback
Speech-to-Text Tools (NaturalReader, Google Read Aloud)	Converts text to speech	Hearing errors and flow

4. Self-Editing Workflow

- **First Pass: Content Check** – Ensure chapters flow logically.
- **Second Pass: Style Check** – Review sentence structure, tone, readability.
- **Third Pass: Proofing** – Correct grammar, spelling, and typos.
- **Final Review: Tools + Human** – Use editing software, then ask a peer to review.

Tip: Don't edit immediately after writing. Wait a day or two for a "fresh eye."

Activity: Build Your Self-Editing Checklist

Step 1: Create Your Own Checklist

Editing Step	Tools / Techniques I Will Use	Timeline
Content Check		
Style Check		
Proofing		
Final Review		

Step 2: Reflection Prompt

"The self-editing techniques I find most useful are _____ because they help me _____. My editing routine will include _____ to make sure my book is professional."

Lesson 3: When & How to Work with Editors

1. Why Work with an Editor?

An editor helps transform your manuscript from good to professional. Even skilled writers benefit from an objective, trained eye. Editors bring clarity, fix blind spots, and prepare your book for publishing standards.

Key Insight: A well-edited book increases reader trust, reviews, and long-term sales.

2. When to Hire an Editor

Stage	Best Time to Work with an Editor	Purpose
Developmental Editing	After completing your first draft	Fix structure, plot holes, and flow
Line Editing	After big-picture issues are solved	Refine style, tone, and readability
Copyediting / Proofreading	Final draft, before publishing	Catch grammar, typos, and formatting issues

Don't send a messy first draft. Do your **self-editing first** (Lesson 2).

3. Types of Editors & What They Do

Type of Editor	Focus	Example of Their Work
Developmental Editor	Structure & story flow	Suggests cutting or adding chapters
Line Editor	Sentence quality	Rewrites clunky sentences for clarity
Copyeditor	Grammar & accuracy	Fixes errors, ensures style guide consistency
Proofreader	Final polish	Finds last typos before publishing

4. How to Find & Work With Editors

Where to Find Them:

- Freelance marketplaces (Upwork, Fiverr, Reedsy)
- Writer networks & associations
- Local editor guilds or publishing services

How to Work Effectively:

- **Research & Vet** – Check samples, reviews, and expertise in your genre.
- **Request a Sample Edit** – Most editors will edit a few pages before you commit.
- **Set Clear Expectations** – Agree on scope (developmental, line, copyedit), timeline, and fees.
- **Communicate Clearly** – Be open to feedback but maintain your author's voice.
- **Budget Wisely** – Editing costs vary. Allocate funds early in your publishing plan.

Activity: Editor Readiness Checklist

Step 1: Is My Manuscript Ready?

Question	Yes/No	Notes
Have I completed at least one full draft?		
Have I done a self-edit for structure & style?		
Is my manuscript free of obvious typos/errors?		
Do I know what type of editing I need?		

Step 2: My Plan for Working With an Editor

Step	Action	Timeline	Budget
1	Research editors		
2	Request sample edit		
3	Hire & communicate clearly		
4	Revise after feedback		

Step 3: Reflection Statement

"The type of editing I need most right now is _____ because _____. My plan for working with an editor will ensure my book is _____ before publishing."

Lesson 4: Beta Readers & Feedback Circles

1. Why Beta Readers Matter

Beta readers are your test audience. They read your manuscript before publishing and give feedback on clarity, pacing, engagement, and overall reader experience.

📌 **Key Insight:** Beta readers are not editors—but they help identify blind spots and give you a sense of how your target readers will respond.

2. What Beta Readers Can Do

Focus Area	What They Check	Example Feedback
Story & Flow	Plot holes, pacing, character development	"Chapter 5 felt rushed compared to earlier chapters."
Clarity	Confusing sections or missing explanations	"I didn't understand why the main character left town."
Engagement	Reader interest, emotional impact	"I loved the twist in Chapter 8—it shocked me!"
Consistency	Tense, names, facts, settings	"You called the teacher Mr. Dube in Chapter 2 and Mr. Duma in Chapter 6."

3. Choosing & Managing Beta Readers

Who Makes a Good Beta Reader?

- Someone from your target audience
- Honest and willing to give constructive feedback
- Not afraid to point out weak spots
- Ideally 3–7 readers for balanced input

Where to Find Them:

- Writing groups & online forums
- Social media communities (Facebook groups, Reddit, Discord)
- Trusted friends who enjoy your genre (but not only family—they may be biased!)

How to Manage Feedback:

- Set clear guidelines (what kind of feedback you want).
- Give them a realistic deadline (2–4 weeks).
- Provide a feedback form or checklist.
- Collect responses and look for patterns.
- Decide what to apply—you remain the author.

4. Feedback Circles

A feedback circle is a small group of writers who exchange drafts and give feedback to each other.

- Encourages accountability.
- Provides diverse perspectives.
- Can be free (peer exchange) or formal (writing workshops).

Activity: Beta Reader Plan

Step 1: Identify Potential Beta Readers

Name	Connection	Why They're a Good Fit	Contacted (Y/N)

Step 2: Design My Feedback Form

Question to Ask Beta Readers	Purpose
Which parts of the book did you enjoy most?	Identify strengths

Were there sections that felt slow or confusing?	Spot weaknesses
Did the characters feel real and consistent?	Check development
Did you notice any inconsistencies (names, dates, events)?	Ensure continuity
Would you recommend this book to a friend? Why/Why not?	Gauge market potential

Step 3: Reflection Statement

"My beta reader strategy will help me improve _____ in my book. I will gather feedback from _____ people and use it to strengthen _____ before moving to final editing."

Lesson 5: Proofreading Basics

1. Why Proofreading Is Essential

Proofreading is the **final polish** before publishing. It ensures your manuscript is free from typos, grammar slips, and formatting errors that can distract readers.

Key Insight: Even small mistakes can hurt your book's credibility. Proofreading is about professionalism and reader trust.

2. What Proofreading Covers

Area	What to Check	Example
Spelling	Typos, homophones	"there" vs. "their"
Grammar	Sentence structure, subject-verb agreement	"She run fast" → "She runs fast"
Punctuation	Commas, quotation marks, apostrophes	"Its" vs. "It's"
Formatting	Page numbers, spacing, font consistency	Chapter headings aligned
Consistency	Character names, tense, facts	"Johannesburg" vs. "Joburg"
Numbers & Dates	Style consistency (10 vs. ten)	"August 20th, 2025" vs. "20 August 2025"

3. Proofreading Strategies

- **Take a Break** – Wait at least a few days after editing before proofreading.
- **Read Aloud** – Helps you catch awkward flow and missing words.
- **Print It Out** – Errors often stand out on paper.
- **Check One Type at a Time** – First spelling, then punctuation, then formatting.
- **Use Tools, But Don't Rely Only on Them** – Grammarly, Word spellcheck, ProWritingAid can help but may miss context errors.
- **Change the Format** – Read your text on a different device or in a different font.

4. Proofreading vs. Editing

Editing	Proofreading
Improves content, flow, and clarity	Corrects surface-level errors
May involve rewriting	Focuses on accuracy
Happens earlier	Final step before publishing

Activity: Proofreading Practice

Step 1: Create Your Personal Proofreading Checklist

Task	Completed (✓)
Check spelling (names, places, common typos)	
Check punctuation (commas, quotes, apostrophes)	
Ensure consistency in tense & voice	
Verify formatting & layout	
Double-check numbers, dates, and names	

Step 2: Test Yourself

Proofread this short example sentence (deliberately incorrect):

> *She walk to the park, it was a long long walk but she didn't stop until she reach her friends house*
> **Rewrite it correctly below:**

Step 3: Reflection Statement

> *"The proofreading strategies I will use most are _____ because they help me _____. I will apply my checklist to ensure my book is polished and ready for publishing."*

End-of-Module Wrap-Up: Reflection & Next Steps

1. Reflect on Your Progress

Take a moment to review what you've achieved in this module. Use the prompts below to guide your reflection:

Reflection Question	My Response
Have I applied self-editing tools & techniques to my manuscript?	
Do I understand the different levels of editing and when to apply them?	
Am I ready to work with editors, or do I need more self-revision first?	
Have I planned how to use beta readers & feedback circles effectively?	
Have I created and used my proofreading checklist?	

2. Celebrate Your Achievements

- Understand the levels of editing (developmental, line, copyediting, proofreading).

- Apply self-editing techniques and tools to strengthen your draft.
- Identify when and how to work with editors professionally.
- Organize and benefit from beta readers & feedback circles.
- Apply proofreading basics to polish your manuscript.

Encouragement:

> *"Your manuscript is no longer just a draft—it's on its way to becoming a professional book."*

3. Next Steps

- **Finalize Your Self-Editing**
  Use your checklist to complete one more review.
- **Decide on Professional Editing**
  Choose the type of editor you need most.
  Research and set a budget.
- **Organize Beta Readers**
  Recruit 3–7 people from your target audience.
  Prepare your feedback form.
- **Proofread with Fresh Eyes**
  Take a short break, then do a final proofread.

4. Reflection Statement

> *"After completing Module 2, I feel more confident about _____. My manuscript is currently _____, and my next step is to _____ before moving into publishing preparation."*

MODULE 3: BOOK DESIGN & FORMATTING

Learning Outcomes

By the end of this module, learners will:

- Understand the structure and anatomy of a book.
- Design professional book covers (DIY or outsourcing).
- Format their manuscript for both print and digital publishing.
- Use tools and templates for clean layouts.

Lesson 1: Anatomy of a Book

1. What Is the Anatomy of a Book?

A book isn't just chapters of text—it's a carefully structured product designed to guide, engage, and satisfy the reader. Each section serves a purpose: some provide context, others add credibility, and others enhance usability.

Think of your book like a **house**:

- The **front matter** is the doorway and welcome mat.
- The **body** is the living space where the story or content happens.
- The **back** matter is the extra rooms, storage, and references for readers who want more.

2. Key Parts of a Book

A. Front Matter (Before the main text)
- Usually numbered in Roman numerals (I, ii, iii…).
- **Title Page** – book title, subtitle, author name, publisher.
- **Copyright Page** – copyright statement, ISBN, disclaimer, publishing info.
- **Dedication (Optional)** – personal message to someone special.
- **Acknowledgments (Optional)** – thanking contributors or supporters.
- **Table of Contents** – navigation for the reader.
- **Foreword (Optional)** – written by someone other than the author.

- **Preface/Introduction** – why the book was written, what to expect.

B. Body (The main content)
- Numbered in Arabic numerals (1, 2, 3…).
- **Chapters / Sections** – organized structure of your book's content.
- **Part Openers (Optional)** – divisions for larger works.
- **Sidebars, Illustrations, Charts (Optional)** – for non-fiction clarity.

C. Back Matter (After the main text)
- Adds value, credibility, and extra support.
- **Epilogue / Conclusion** – wrapping up the narrative or message.
- **Appendices** – additional information or resources.
- **Glossary** – definitions of special terms.
- **Bibliography / References** – credibility for non-fiction.
- **Index** – alphabetical listing of topics.
- **About the Author** – author bio, photo, and next steps for readers.
- **Acknowledgments** (sometimes placed here too).

3. Why This Matters for You
- Creates **professional credibility.**
- Improves **reader navigation** and satisfaction.
- Meets **publishing standards** (important for print and eBook).
- Makes your book **market-ready.**

Reflection Prompt
- Which parts of the anatomy do I already have in my draft?
- Which parts do I need to add to make my book complete?

Encouragement:

> ➤ "A book isn't just words—it's an experience. By learning its anatomy, you're preparing to present your work like a true professional author."

Lesson 2: Cover Design

1. Why Book Covers Matter

- **First impression** = lasting impression. A cover is often the first—and sometimes only—thing a reader sees before deciding to buy.
- **It's not just art**—it's marketing. Covers communicate genre, tone, and professionalism instantly.
- **Readers DO judge a book by its cover.**

2. Anatomy of a Book Cover

Front Cover:

- Title (bold, clear, readable in thumbnail size).
- Subtitle (optional – clarifies theme/niche).
- Author name (your brand).
- Visuals/graphics (match book's tone).
- Balanced layout (color, typography, spacing).

Spine (print books):

- Title.
- Author name.
- Publisher logo (if applicable).

Back Cover:

- Blurb/synopsis (short, compelling).
- Endorsements/reviews (optional).
- Barcode/ISBN (required for retail).
- Author bio + photo (optional).

3. Key Principles of Good Cover Design

- Clarity over complexity.
- Match your genre.
- Professional typography.
- Consistent branding.

- Thumbnail readability.

4. How to Create a Cover
- **DIY Tools:** Canva, BookBrush, Adobe Express, Affinity Publisher, Photoshop.
- **Professional Help:** Fiverr, Upwork, 99Designs, cover design studios.

Tip: Even if self-publishing, investing in a professional cover pays off.

Activity: Cover Design Planning

Step	Task	Notes
1	Write down your **working title and subtitle**	
2	Identify your **genre** and research 2–3 bestselling covers in that niche	
3	Sketch or describe your **ideal cover concept** (colors, imagery, mood)	
4	Decide: DIY design or hire a professional? Why?	

Reflection Questions
- What message should my cover instantly communicate?
- Do I need professional help, or can I design it myself with the right tools?

Encouragement:

> "Your book cover is not just decoration—it's your book's handshake with the world. Make it firm, confident, and unforgettable."

Lesson 3: Formatting for Print

1. Why Print Formatting Matters

- A poorly formatted book feels unprofessional and distracts readers.
- Proper formatting ensures readability, credibility, and acceptance by print-on-demand services (Amazon KDP, IngramSpark, local printers).
- Good design = a smoother reader experience.

2. Key Print Formatting Elements

a) Trim Size (Book Dimensions)

Common sizes:

- 5" x 8" (popular for fiction).
- 6" x 9" (common for non-fiction/self-help).
- A5 (148 x 210 mm, often used locally).

Choose based on your genre and printing cost.

b) Margins & Bleed

- **Margins:** Leave enough white space for readability (at least 0.5–0.75 inches).
- **Gutter Margin:** Extra space on the inside (spine side) to prevent text disappearing.
- **Bleed:** Extend images/graphics slightly beyond the edge for clean printing.

c) Fonts & Text Layout

- **Body Text:** Serif fonts (e.g., Times New Roman, Garamond, Georgia).
- **Headings:** Bold serif or sans-serif for contrast.
- **Font Size:** Usually 11–12 pt for readability.
- **Line Spacing:** 1.15–1.5 for clean flow.
- **Paragraphs:** Indent first line OR use spacing—but not both.

d) Front & Back Matter

- **Front Matter:** Title page, copyright page, dedication, table of contents, preface/introduction.
- **Back Matter:** Author bio, acknowledgments, references, ads for other books, index (if relevant).

3. Tools for Print Formatting

- **Microsoft Word:** Simple, but limited for complex layouts.
- **Google Docs:** Useful draft tool, less control for print.
- **Vellum (Mac only):** Easy book formatting.
- **Atticus** (cross-platform, alternative to Vellum).
- **Adobe InDesign:** Professional publishing standard.

Activity: Print Layout Planning

Step	Task	Notes
1	Choose your **book trim size** (5x8, 6x9, A5, etc.)	
2	Set your **margins & gutter** in your word processor	
3	Select a **body font & size** (e.g., Garamond, 12 pt)	
4	List what you'll include in your **front and back matter**	

Reflection Questions

- Does my chosen trim size suit my genre and audience?
- Am I confident with DIY formatting, or should I use a tool/professional?

Encouragement:

> "A well-formatted book is like a well-tailored suit—it makes your words shine with professionalism and style."

Lesson 4: Formatting for Digital

Why Digital Formatting Matters

In today's publishing world, digital books (eBooks) are not just optional—they're essential. Millions of readers consume stories and knowledge through e-readers, tablets, and even smartphones. A poorly formatted eBook can frustrate readers, while a professionally formatted one enhances readability, accessibility, and overall satisfaction.

Unlike print, where fixed layouts dominate, eBooks require **flexible, reflowable design** that adapts to different screen sizes and reading apps. That means less focus on page numbers, and more on **flow, structure, and navigation**.

Key Elements of Digital Book Formatting

1. File Types & Platforms

- **EPUB** → Most widely supported (Apple Books, Kobo, Google Play Books).
- **MOBI** (legacy) → Previously used for Kindle; now replaced by KPF (Kindle Package Format).
- **PDF** → Fixed layout, not ideal for reflowable text but still used for workbooks or manuals.

Most self-publishing platforms (like **Amazon KDP**) will accept an EPUB upload.

2. Structure & Layout

- **No page numbers** → e-readers generate their own.
- **Consistent headings** → Use styles (Heading 1, Heading 2) to make chapters clickable.
- **Simple fonts** → Readers can adjust fonts, so stick to defaults like Times, Arial, Georgia.
- **Line spacing & alignment** → Avoid double spaces, justify text where possible.

3. Navigation & Metadata

- **Clickable Table of Contents** → Essential for easy navigation.
- **Metadata** → Includes title, author, keywords, description. This helps search engines and bookstores display your book correctly.
- **Hyperlinks** → Add links to your website, social media, or references.

4. Images & Media

- Use high-resolution images (300 dpi) but compress for digital to avoid large file sizes.
- Center images and avoid wrapping text around them.
- For fixed-layout children's books, cookbooks, or comics → use PDF or special EPUB formats.

5. Testing & Proofing

- Always preview your eBook on different devices (Kindle Previewer, Apple Books, Adobe Digital Editions).
- Check for spacing issues, broken links, and image placement.

6. Tools for Digital Formatting

- **Scrivener** – Writing + exporting to eBook.
- **Vellum (Mac only)** – Simple drag-and-drop formatting for EPUB & Kindle.
- **Calibre** – Free tool for converting between eBook formats.
- **Reedsy Book Editor** – Free, browser-based tool for professional eBook creation.

7. Quick Example

Imagine your book is uploaded as a PDF with fixed margins. On a small phone screen, readers must zoom in and scroll side-to-side—frustrating!

But if it's properly formatted as an EPUB, the text **reflows** beautifully, font sizes can be adjusted, and the experience is seamless.

Activity: Digital Formatting Checklist

Task: Take your manuscript and check if it meets these requirements:

Meets Requirements	Yes	No
Does it use proper heading styles (for TOC navigation)?		
Are all chapters starting on a new page (section breaks)?		

Have you tested your file in at least two different eBook readers?		
Is metadata (title, author, description) filled out?		
Did you keep fonts simple and consistent?		

- If you can check off all these items, your eBook is **reader-friendly and platform-ready.**

Key Takeaway

Formatting for digital is about **flexibility, readability, and accessibility.** While print demands precision, digital demands adaptability. The smoother the reading experience, the more likely readers will finish—and love—your book.

Lesson 5: Polishing the Final Layout

1. Why the Final Layout Matters

Your manuscript is written, edited, and formatted — but before publishing, you must give it a **final polish**. This stage is about ensuring your book looks professional, flows smoothly, and is free of distracting errors or inconsistencies. Think of it as the last "shine" before placing your work in readers' hands.

This step is not about rewriting—it's about **quality assurance.** A well-polished layout helps your book stand shoulder-to-shoulder with traditionally published titles.

2. Key Elements of Polishing

2.1 Consistency Check

- Font type, size, and spacing should be uniform.
- Chapter titles, subtitles, and headings must follow the same style.

- Ensure margins, indents, and line spacing are consistent throughout.

2.2 Front & Back Matter Review

- Title page: clean, correct, professional.
- Copyright page: accurate details.
- Dedication, Preface, and Acknowledgments: properly placed.
- Back matter: Author bio, "About the Author," and links should be neat and clickable (digital).

2.3 Typography & Spacing

- Avoid widows (single word on a line) and orphans (single line on a page).
- Ensure proper spacing after punctuation (one space after periods, not two).
- Check alignment: justified text should not create rivers (big gaps).

2. 4 Image & Graphic Check

- Ensure all images are sharp (300 dpi for print).
- Captions match the image placement.
- No images stretch awkwardly across devices (for eBooks).

2.5. Final Proof

- Read your book in **both print and digital previewers.**
- Check hyperlinks (for digital).
- Print a sample proof copy from your print-on-demand service (like Amazon KDP or IngramSpark).
- Print a sample proof copy from your print-on-demand service (like Amazon KDP or IngramSpark).

Example

Imagine a reader picks up your book and notices:

- Some chapters start halfway down the page.
- Fonts change randomly.
- A typo in the title page!

This creates an impression of carelessness. But when polished, everything flows seamlessly, giving your book the **professional touch it deserves.**

Activity: Final Layout Polishing Checklist

Manuscript Meet Requirements	Yes	No
Fonts and headings are consistent.		
No widows, orphans, or awkward spacing.		
Front and back matter are correctly placed.		
Images are high quality and correctly positioned.		
Digital version tested on Kindle/Apple Books/other devices.		
Print proof copy reviewed.		

Key Takeaway

Polishing the final layout is your last **line of defence** before publishing. It's the moment where you ensure your book doesn't just read well—it **looks and feels professional.** Readers might forgive a small typo, but they will notice messy formatting. A polished layout communicates respect for your craft and your audience.

End-of-Module Wrap-Up

Congratulations — you've completed **Book Design & Formatting!** At this stage, your manuscript is no longer just words on a page; it is transforming into a **professional book ready for readers worldwide.**

Reflection Questions

Take a moment to reflect on your progress:

- Do you understand the **anatomy of a book** (front matter, body, back matter)?

- Have you experimented with different **cover design ideas?**
- Did you practice formatting for **print** and **digital** versions
- Have you created a **final polishing checklist** to ensure professional quality?

Activity: Personal Progress Journal

Write down in your learner's journal:

- What was the most exciting part of designing your book (cover, formatting, or layout)?
- What challenges do you think you'll face in book design, and how will you overcome them?
- How confident do you feel now about making your book look professional

Encouragement

Remember:

A book is not only judged by its story—it's also judged by its appearance.

You now have the tools to make your book look and **feel like a bestseller** from page one to the very last word.

You are no longer just a writer — you are also a **book designer in progress.**

MODULE 4: PUBLISHING PLATFORMS & DISTRIBUTION

Learning Outcomes

By the end of this module, learners will:

- Understand the differences between self-publishing and traditional publishing.
- Compare major publishing platforms (Amazon KDP, IngramSpark, Draft2Digital, Smashwords, Lulu, etc.).
- Learn how to set up accounts and upload files.
- Explore distribution options (print, eBook, audiobook).
- Make informed choices about global reach vs. niche/local publishing.

Lesson 1: Publishing Pathways

1. Why Publishing Pathways Matter

Writing and formatting your book is only half the journey — now comes the critical step of **choosing the right pathway to publish and distribute** it. Each pathway (print, digital, audio) offers unique advantages, challenges, and audiences. Successful authors often use a combination to **maximize reach and earnings**.

2. Publishing Pathways

2.1 Print Publishing (Paperback & Hardcover)

Pros:

- Tangible product readers can hold.
- Higher perceived value (many readers still prefer print).
- Great for signings, events, and local sales.

Cons:

- Printing costs.
- Distribution may be limited if not using global POD (Print on Demand).

- Platforms: Amazon KDP, IngramSpark, Lulu.

2.2 Digital Publishing (eBooks)

Pros:

- Instant global reach.
- No printing costs.
- Easy updates and edits.
- Accessible to mobile/tablet users worldwide.

Cons:

- Lower retail prices than print.
- Some markets still prefer print.
- Formats: EPUB, MOBI, PDF.
- Platforms: Amazon Kindle, Apple Books, Kobo, Google Play Books.

2.3 Audio Publishing (Audiobooks)

Pros:

- Fastest-growing sector in publishing.
- Reaches multitaskers (drivers, gym-goers, busy professionals).
- Adds an extra revenue stream.

Cons:

- Requires narration and production (can be costly).
- Larger file sizes, slower uploads.
- Platforms: ACX (Audible), Findaway Voices, Kobo Audiobooks.

3. Example Scenario

Imagine an author in South Africa writing a motivational guide. They release:

- Print version for workshops and book fairs.
- eBook version for global sales on Amazon and Kobo.
- Audiobook version narrated by themselves for a personal connection.
- This multi-pathway approach triples their reach and revenue streams.

Activity: Publishing Pathway Choice

In your learner's journal, answer:

- Which publishing pathway do you see as your primary focus (print, digital, or audio)?
- Which additional format could you add later to expand your reach?
- What excites you most about exploring different pathways?

Key Takeaway

Each publishing pathway opens doors to **different audiences and opportunities.** There's no "one right way." The most successful authors think **strategically** and often combine print, digital, and audio to build a strong publishing presence.

Lesson 2: Major Self-Publishing Platforms

1. Why Platforms Matter

Choosing where to publish your book is just as important as writing it. The platform you choose determines your **audience reach, royalties, and distribution network.** Some platforms dominate the global market, while others specialize in niche audiences or regional distribution. Understanding the strengths of each helps you make informed choices.

2. Major Self-Publishing Platforms

2.1 Amazon Kindle Direct Publishing (KDP)

Strengths:

- World's largest self-publishing platform.
- Distribution to Kindle (eBook) and Amazon Print (POD).
- Global audience across multiple countries.
- Up to 70% royalties (depending on pricing).

Limitations:

- Very competitive marketplace.

- Some countries may have limited access.

2.2 IngramSpark

Strengths:

- Huge print distribution network (bookstores, libraries).
- Professional-quality printing (hardcover & paperback).
- Complementary to Amazon KDP (not competing).

Limitations:

- Setup fees for publishing & revisions.
- More technical formatting requirements.

2.3 Apple Books, Kobo, & Google Play Books

- **Apple Books:** Reaches Apple device users worldwide.
- **Kobo:** Strong presence in Canada, Europe, and Asia.
- **Google Play Books:** Powerful integration with Android devices.

Strengths: Alternative audiences outside Amazon, often less crowded.

Limitations: Smaller market share compared to Amazon.

2.4 Smashwords / Draft2Digital

Strengths:

- Wide distribution (aggregator) to multiple platforms.
- Easy publishing interface.
- Useful for reaching platforms like Barnes & Noble, OverDrive (libraries), and niche retailers.

Limitations:

- Slightly lower royalties since they take a share as aggregator.

2.5 ACX / Findaway Voices (Audiobooks)

Strengths:

- ACX connects directly to Audible and iTunes.

- Findaway distributes to 40+ audiobook retailers.

Limitations:

- Audiobook production costs (if you don't narrate yourself).

2.6 Local & Regional Platforms (South Africa example)

- Ethnikids (Children's books with African focus).
- Snapplify & African eBook distributors.
- Direct publishing via your own website

Strength: Local visibility, cultural alignment.

Limitation: Smaller audience size than global platforms.

Example Scenario

An author could:

- Use **Amazon KDP** for global eBook & POD reach.
- Add **IngramSpark** for bookstore/library distribution.
- Publish an **audiobook via ACX** for Audible listeners.
- Offer a **direct digital copy** on their own website for loyal fans.

This combination builds **global + local** presence.

Activity: Platform Mapping

In your learner's journal:

- Which platform feels like the best fit for your first book?
- How could you combine platforms to reach different audiences?
- Would you consider local/regional publishing in addition to global?

Key Takeaway

No single platform is enough. Smart authors use a **multi-platform strategy** to maximize their reach, royalties, and impact. The goal is to balance **global visibility** with **local connection.**

Lesson 3: Uploading Your Book

1. Why Uploading Matters

After writing, editing, and formatting, the next big milestone is **uploading your manuscript to a publishing platform.** This process is more than just dragging and dropping a file — it involves **technical requirements, metadata, and presentation choices** that influence how readers discover and purchase your book.

2. The Uploading Process (Step-by-Step)

2.1 Prepare Your Files

- **Manuscript:** PDF for print, EPUB for eBook, MP3/WAV for audio.
- **Cover Design:** High-resolution (300 dpi for print, JPG/PNG for eBook).
- **Additional Assets:** Author photo, book description (blurb), keywords.

2.2 Set Up Your Account

- Create an author account on your chosen platform (e.g., Amazon KDP, IngramSpark).
- Add tax and banking details for royalties.

2.3 Enter Book Details (Metadata)

- **Title & Subtitle** – must match exactly with your manuscript.
- **Author Name** – consistent across your book and platform.
- **Book Description (Blurb)** – compelling, reader-focused summary.
- **Keywords** – 7–10 terms readers might search for.
- **Categories** – choose genres and sub-genres carefully.

2.4 Upload Interior & Cover Files

- Upload formatted manuscript file.
- Upload front cover (and full wrap cover for print).
- Check previews on both digital and print previewers.

2.5 Set Pricing & Royalties

- Choose royalty options (e.g., 35% vs 70% on Amazon).
- Decide global pricing (convert to different currencies).
- Consider free promotions or discounts for launch.

2.6 Review & Publish

- Preview your book in digital and print simulators.
- Fix formatting issues before hitting "Publish."
- Submit for approval (may take 24–72 hours depending on the platform).

3. Example Scenario

An author uploads their eBook on **Amazon KDP:**

- Uploads a clean EPUB file and a 300 dpi cover.
- Selects "Business & Self-Help" as the main category.
- Adds keywords: self-publishing, writing guide, book marketing.
- Sets the price at **$3.99 eBook / $12.99 print.**
- Within 48 hours, the book is live on Amazon globally.

Activity: Uploading Checklist

In your learner's journal, list the items you will need when you upload your book:

Items Completed	Yes	No
Manuscript file (formatted).		
Cover design (correct dimensions).		
Blurb and author bio.		
Keywords and categories.		
Pricing strategy.		

Key Takeaway

Uploading your book is not just about "going live" — it's about **presenting your book to the world in the best possible way.** The care you put into your files, metadata, and pricing will directly influence your book's discoverability and sales.

Lesson 4: Distribution Options

1. Why Distribution Matters

Publishing your book is just the first step. **Distribution determines how and where readers can actually access your work.** A book that is "published but not distributed" is like a song no one can hear — it exists, but it doesn't reach its audience. Understanding your distribution options helps you balance **reach, control, and royalties.**

2. Distribution Pathways

2.1 Amazon-Only Distribution

- Your book is available exclusively through Amazon.

Pros: Simplicity, higher royalty options (70% eBooks in certain regions), access to Kindle Unlimited (subscription readers).

Cons: Limits reach outside the Amazon ecosystem.

2.2 Wide Distribution (Multi-Platform)

- Your book is distributed across many retailers (Apple, Kobo, Google, libraries).

Pros: Wider global reach, avoids dependence on one platform.

Cons: Lower royalties on some sales, more complex setup.

2.3 Print-on-Demand (POD)

- Books are printed when ordered (Amazon KDP Print, IngramSpark, Lulu).

Pros: No inventory costs, global print distribution, eco-friendly.

Cons: Lower margins per book compared to bulk printing.

2.4 Local & Regional Distribution

- Partnering with bookstores, libraries, cultural organizations, or local platforms (e.g., Snapplify in South Africa).

Pros: Strong local visibility, supports community literacy.

Cons: Limited international exposure unless combined with global distribution.

2.5 Direct-to-Consumer Sales

- Selling books directly via your own website, social media, or at events.

Pros: Highest royalties (no middleman), direct relationship with readers, ability to bundle (book + course, etc.).

Cons: Requires your own marketing, payment setup, and shipping (for print).

3. Example Scenario

A South African author could:

- Use **Amazon KDP** for global reach.
- Add **IngramSpark** for library/bookstore distribution.
- Partner with **local bookstores & schools** to reach nearby readers.
- Sell signed copies via their own website.

This layered approach creates **both international and local presence.**

Activity: Distribution Mapping

In your learner's journal, answer:

- Do you want to start **Amazon**-only or go wide immediately?
- Would **Print-on-Demand** or local printing make more sense for your book?
- How might you include **direct-to-consumer** sales as part of your strategy?

Key Takeaway

Distribution is where your book leaves your hands and enters the world. Smart authors mix global platforms, local opportunities, and direct sales to **maximize reach and income.** Think of it as building multiple doors for readers to find you.

Lesson 5: Pricing & Royalties

1. Why Pricing & Royalties Matter

Pricing is more than just a number — it determines how accessible your book is to readers and how much you earn per sale. Royalties are the **percentage of the selling price you keep** after the distributor takes their share. Getting these right ensures your book is **competitive, profitable, and sustainable.**

2. Key Pricing Considerations

2.1 Genre & Market Norms

- Novels often sell lower (especially eBooks) than academic or professional books.

Example: eBook fiction ($2.99–$6.99), nonfiction/professional ($5.99–$14.99).

2.2 Format Matters

- **eBooks**: Lower price, high volume.
- **Paperbacks/Hardcovers:** Higher price, but higher production costs.
- **Audiobooks**: Often priced higher due to recording costs.

2.3 Audience & Goals

Are you aiming for maximum reach (lower pricing) or higher income per sale (premium pricing)?

3. Understanding Royalties

3.1 Amazon Kindle Direct Publishing (KDP)

eBooks:

- 70% royalty for books priced $2.99–$9.99 (in eligible regions).
- 35% royalty for books below $2.99 or above $9.99.
- Paperbacks: Around 60% royalty minus printing costs.

3.2 Other Platforms (Apple, Kobo, Google, etc.)

- Usually 70% royalty on eBooks, but rules differ slightly.

3.3 IngramSpark (Print Distribution)

- About 40–50% royalty after retailer discounts + printing costs.

3.4 Direct-to-Consumer Sales

- 100% royalty (minus payment gateway fees, e.g., PayPal or card fees).
- You keep the most here, but marketing is fully your responsibility.

4. Example Breakdown

- eBook price: **$4.99 on Amazon**
- Royalty (70%): **$3.49 per copy**
- Paperback price: **$14.99 POD via KDP**
- Printing cost: **$4.50**
- Royalty (60% after printing): **$4.49 per copy**

Direct sale paperback (same $14.99, sold via your website)

- Printing cost: **$4.50**
- Payment fee: **$0.50**
- Royalty: **$9.99 per copy**

Notice how direct sales nearly double your earnings compared to Amazon.

5. Pricing Strategies

- **Introductory Pricing** – Start low to attract early readers, then raise later.
- **Tiered Pricing** – Offer different editions (e.g., eBook cheaper, paperback mid-range, signed hardcover premium).
- **Localized Pricing** – Adjust price for different markets (e.g., South Africa vs. US) for affordability.
- **Value Bundles** – Sell the book with a course, workbook, or signed copy for higher value.

Activity: Pricing Your Book

1. Draft a possible **eBook price** and **print price** for your book.

2. Calculate approximate royalties per sale.

3. Reflect: Do you want to prioritize **reach** (lower price) or **profit margin** (higher price)?

Key Takeaway

Pricing and royalties are a balancing act between **reader affordability, global market expectations, and your income goals.** Don't underprice your work, but also don't price yourself out of your audience's reach.

End-of-Module Wrap-Up

1. What You've Learned

In this module, you explored the **entire landscape of publishing platforms and distribution**, from making the big decision of how to publish, to actually pricing and preparing your book for readers. You now understand:

- **Publishing Pathways** – The differences between traditional publishing, self-publishing, and hybrid models, and which path suits your goals.
- **Major Self-Publishing Platforms** – Amazon KDP, IngramSpark, Apple Books, Kobo, and more — what each offers.
- **Uploading Your Book** – Step-by-step overview of preparing and submitting your manuscript.
- **Distribution Options** – Global reach through distributors, direct sales, bookstores, and libraries.
- **Pricing & Royalties** – How to strategically set your book's price while understanding your earnings.

2. Why This Matters

Publishing is no longer a mystery. You now have the knowledge to:

- Confidently choose a publishing route.

- Navigate platforms like a pro.
- Set competitive prices while maximizing royalties.
- Distribute your book worldwide — or directly to your audience.

This knowledge puts you in the **driver's seat of your publishing journey**, with flexibility and full creative control.

End-of-Module Activity

Create Your Publishing Plan

1. Decide on your preferred publishing pathway (traditional, self, or hybrid).

2. Choose two platforms you'd like to publish on and note why.

3. Draft your initial pricing (ebook + print) and calculate your royalty expectations.

4. Write down your primary distribution goal: global reach, niche/local focus, or direct sales.

Key Takeaway

Your book is not just a manuscript anymore — it's becoming a **product ready for the world**. Knowing how to publish, distribute, and price it ensures your hard work finds its audience and earns you the recognition (and income) you deserve.

MODULE 5: MARKETING & AUDIENCE BUILDING

Learning Outcomes

By the end of this module, learners will:

- Understand how to position their book in the market.
- Learn strategies to grow an engaged audience before and after launch.
- Create a marketing plan tailored to their book and audience.
- Use digital tools for promotion (social media, email marketing, ads).
- Build an author brand for long-term success.

Lesson 1: The Author as a Brand

Core Content

1. What Does It Mean to Be a Brand?

A brand is not just a logo or name — it's the **perception people have of you**. For authors, your brand includes:

- Your writing style and themes.
- Your personality and online presence.
- The emotional connection readers feel with you.
- A strong brand creates **trust, recognition, and loyalty.**

2. Why Author Branding Matters

- **Visibility**: Makes you stand out in a crowded market.
- **Connection**: Builds relationships with readers.
- **Consistency**: Readers know what to expect from your work.
- **Longevity**: A strong brand keeps readers returning for every book you release.

3. Core Elements of an Author Brand

- **Voice & Message:** The tone and values reflected in your books and communication.
- **Visual Identity:** Colors, fonts, book cover style, website/social media look.
- **Niche & Genre Positioning:** Clarity about who your readers are and what you offer them.
- **Author Bio & Story:** Your journey as a writer — this makes you relatable and memorable.

4. Examples of Author Branding

- **J.K. Rowling** → Magical worlds, detailed lore, imaginative wonder.
- **Chimamanda Ngozi Adichie** → Powerful storytelling about culture, feminism, and identity.
- **Trevor Noah** → Humor, resilience, and South African identity.

Each one stands out because their **name itself carries meaning**. That is the power of branding.

Activity: Define Your Brand

Take a notebook or journal and answer these questions:

- What three words best describe you as a writer?
- What emotions or values do you want readers to feel from your books?
- Who is your ideal reader? (Age, interest, location, values)
- What is one personal story you can share that strengthens your connection with readers?

Write these answers down — this will be the **foundation of your Author Brand Statement.**

Key Takeaway

You are not just an author — you are a **brand**. Your brand is the bridge between your words and your readers' hearts. By building it with intention, you create recognition, trust, and lasting impact.

Lesson 2: Pre-Launch Audience Building

Core Content

1. Why Pre-Launch Matters

Books don't sell just because they exist — they sell because readers are **waiting for them**. A pre-launch strategy ensures that:

Engaging with communities (book clubs, online forums, local networks).

- You're not launching into silence.
- You create buzz and momentum.
- Readers feel like part of your journey from the start.

2. Core Pre-Launch Strategies

- **Start Early:** Begin 6–12 months before release if possible.
- **Email List Building:** Offer a freebie (sample chapter, mini-guide, short story) to encourage sign-ups.
- **Landing Page:** Create a simple page where readers can learn about your book and sign up for updates.
- **Social Media Teasers:** Share snippets, quotes, cover reveals, and progress milestones.
- **Community Engagement:** Join online groups, book clubs, or writing circles related to your genre.

3. Ways to Generate Buzz

- Share your **cover design reveal** as an event.
- Post **behind-the-scenes content** about your writing journey.
- Give out **Advance Reader Copies (ARCs)** to early supporters.
- Run small **giveaways** (signed copies, free ebooks, merchandise).
- Collaborate with **bloggers, podcasters, and book reviewers** for early exposure.

4. Collaborations & Partnerships

- Partner with other indie authors for joint promotions.
- Cross-promote with creators in related niches.
- Build relationships with influencers who can champion your book.

Activity: Your Pre-Launch Blueprint

Answer these questions in your journal/workbook:

- Which platform (social media or email) will you focus on most?

- What freebie could you offer to attract early readers?
- Who could you collaborate with (author friends, reviewers, book clubs)?
- What is one specific date you'll set for your first teaser post?

Key Takeaway

A successful launch begins long before release day. By building anticipation, connecting with readers, and creating excitement, you ensure your book has eager readers waiting when it finally arrives.

Lesson 3: Marketing Tools & Tactics

Core Content

1. Essential Marketing Tools for Authors

- **Email Marketing Platforms** (e.g., Mailchimp, ConvertKit, Sendinblue)
  → Best for building direct, loyal relationships with readers.
- **Author Website / Blog**
  → Your professional "home base" where readers learn about you and your books.
- **Social Media Platforms** (Facebook, Instagram, TikTok, LinkedIn, Twitter/X)
  → Great for reach, engagement, and brand visibility.
- **Design Tools** (Canva, BookBrush)
  → Create professional graphics, teasers, and promo materials.
- **Advertising Tools** (Amazon Ads, Facebook Ads, BookBub Ads)
  → Targeted exposure to book buyers.
- **Analytics Tools** (Google Analytics, platform insights)
  → Track performance and learn what works.

2. Proven Marketing Tactics for Authors

- **Cover Reveal Events:** Generate buzz by making your book's cover reveal a big moment.
- **ARC** (Advance Reader Copy) Campaigns: Send early copies to reviewers and readers to build momentum.

- **Book Launch Team:** Recruit friends, fans, and beta readers to promote your book during launch week.
- **Content Marketing:** Share blog posts, videos, or podcasts about your journey or book theme.
- **Cross-Promotion:** Partner with other authors in your genre to share audiences.
- **Paid Ads:** Start small with targeted ads on Amazon, Facebook, or BookBub.
- **Giveaways & Contests:** Offer signed copies or exclusive content to create excitement.

3. Choosing the Right Tools & Tactics

Not every tool or strategy fits every author. Consider:

- Your **budget** (free vs. paid tools).
- Your **target audience** (where do they spend time online?)
- Your **personal strengths** (do you love writing blogs, making videos, or running ads?).

Activity: Your Marketing Toolbox

Reflect and write down:

- Which **three marketing tools** will you commit to using (email list, website, social media, etc.)?
- Which **two tactics** will you try for your upcoming book launch?
- What is **one small marketing action** you can take this week to start building momentum?

Key Takeaway

Marketing doesn't have to be overwhelming. By focusing on the right tools and simple, effective tactics, you can steadily grow your audience, generate buzz, and set your book up for success.

Lesson 4: Launch Strategies

Core Content

1. What Makes a Successful Launch?

A book launch is your book's **big first impression.** Success depends on:

- Having a **prepared audience** (built during pre-launch).
- Creating **buzz and urgency.**
- Coordinating multiple marketing activities at once.

2. Types of Book Launches

- **Big Splash Launch**
  → Heavy promotion, big announcements, ads, events, giveaways.
  → Best for authors with a strong pre-launch following.
- **Soft Launch**
  → Quiet release with minimal promotion. Focuses on gathering reviews first.
  → Best for first-time authors or testing a market.
- **Hybrid Launch**
  → Begin with a soft launch for reviews, then build up to a big promotional push.

3. Key Launch Strategies

- **Email Announcements:** Send launch emails to your list with links to buy.
- **Social Media Countdown:** Share daily updates (quotes, behind-the-scenes, launch-day celebration).
- **Book Launch Team:** Mobilize supporters to post, review, and spread the word.
- **ARC Reviews:** Ensure reviews are live on Amazon/Goodreads on launch day.
- **Giveaways & Contests:** Create excitement and reward early supporters.
- **Launch Events:** Online launch party (live stream), local bookstore event, or virtual Q&A.
- **Advertising Boost:** Use Amazon/Facebook ads in the first 1–2 weeks to catch new readers.

4. The First 30 Days Matter

Amazon and other platforms reward books that get:

- **High sales velocity** (fast sales at launch).
- **Consistent reviews** (reader trust).
- **Engagement** (mentions, shares, buzz).

Your launch should focus on maximizing all three.

Activity: Design Your Launch Plan

Answer in your journal/workbook:

- Which launch model (big splash, soft, hybrid) suits your current situation?
- What 3 launch activities will you commit to? (e.g., email blast, giveaway, online event)
- Who can be on your **launch team** to help you spread the word?

Key Takeaway

A strong launch gives your book the momentum it needs to succeed. Whether big or small, the key is planning, consistency, and mobilizing readers who believe in your work.

Lesson 5: Post-Launch Growth

Core Content

1. Why Post-Launch Matters

Speaking engagemen

Many authors stop promoting after launch week. But the truth is:

- Long-term growth is where real success lies.
- A steady sales curve builds credibility and income.
- Your first book becomes the foundation for future titles.

2. Post-Launch Growth Strategies

Keep Marketing Alive

- Continue posting book-related content on social media.
- Run occasional promotions or discounts to boost sales.
- Use Amazon Ads or BookBub Ads to keep visibility up.

Leverage Reviews

- Share positive reader reviews on your platforms.
- Encourage new readers to leave reviews by asking at the end of your book.

Engage with Your Readers

- Start a reader newsletter with exclusive content.
- Create bonus material (short stories, deleted scenes, Q&As).
- Build a Facebook group, Discord server, or private community for fans.

Expand Your Reach

- Pitch yourself to podcasts, blogs, and local media.
- Attend book fairs, author events, or online panels.
- Translate your book or create audiobook editions.

Plan for the Next Book

- Begin teasing your next project early.
- Use your current book to lead readers into your next release.
- Remember: the best marketing for a book is another book.

3. Measuring Your Growth

Track:

- Monthly sales numbers.
- Email list growth.
- Social media engagement.
- Review count and average rating.

Use this data to refine your ongoing strategy.

Activity: Post-Launch Roadmap

In your workbook, write down:

- How will you keep your current book visible after launch week?
- What ongoing marketing activity will you commit to (ads, reviews, social media, newsletter)?
- What steps can you take now to begin preparing readers for your next book?

Key Takeaway

A successful launch is only the beginning. True author success comes from **sustained visibility, reader loyalty, and consistent publishing**. Treat each book not as the end, but as a stepping stone toward building your career.

End-of-Module Wrap-Up

You've reached the end of **Module 5: Marketing & Audience Building** — one of the most crucial parts of your author journey. Writing the book is only half the work; building an audience ensures that your words find the right readers.

Key Takeaways

- **You are a brand** – As an author, people connect with you as much as your book.
- **Build early** – Start gathering an audience before launch to create anticipation.
- **Use the right tools** – Social media, newsletters, websites, and collaborations help you reach readers effectively.
- **Launch smart** – A strong launch strategy can make the difference between silence and buzz.
- **Think long-term** – Post-launch growth requires consistency, engagement, and continuous marketing.

Reflective Questions for Learners

1. Do you have a clear sense of your **author brand identity?**

2. Which **audience-building strategies** resonate most with you?

3. Have you chosen your **primary marketing tools** (e.g., social media, email list, author website)?

4. Do you already have ideas for a **launch strategy** that feels right for your book?

5. How will you maintain momentum **after launch?**

Activity: Build Your Marketing Roadmap

Take a fresh page in your notebook (or use a digital tool) and sketch your **Marketing Roadmap:**

Pre-Launch	Launch Week	Post-Launch
How will you build hype before your book is released?	What's your step-by-step plan for maximum visibility?	How will you continue engaging readers and growing your reach?
1.	1.	1.
2.	2.	2.
3.	3.	3.
4.	4.	4.

Tip: Think of this as your book's "GPS system" — it guides you from writing to readers' hands.

Encouragement

Marketing may feel overwhelming, but remember: it's simply sharing your story with people who need it. Every post, every conversation, every small step adds up.

You are not just writing a book; you are building a legacy.

Keep your eyes on your readers — they're waiting for your story.

You are now equipped with the tools to **grow your audience, launch with impact, and sustain your presence as an author.**

MODULE 6: MONETIZATION & LONG-TERM STRATEGY

Learning Outcomes

By the end of this module, learners will:

- Understand multiple income streams from one book.
- Explore how to repurpose content (courses, workshops, merchandise).
- Learn how to protect and manage intellectual property (IP).
- Create a long-term publishing and business strategy.

Lesson 1: Beyond Book Sales

Publishing a book is only the beginning of your author journey. While book sales are important, true success comes when you learn to **expand your income streams** and leverage your book as a platform for other opportunities.

Key Concepts

- **Books as Doors, Not Endpoints**
  Your book opens doors to bigger opportunities: speaking, teaching, coaching, or consulting.
  Selling directly via your website for higher margins.
  Think of your book as your **business card on steroids** — it builds credibility instantly.

- **Workshops & Training**
  Turn your book's lessons into workshops, online courses, or webinars.
  Readers who want deeper insights are willing to pay for structured learning.

- **Speaking Engagements**
  Authors often get invited to speak at conferences, schools, or organizations.
  Speaking fees + book sales at events = double income stream.

- **Licensing & Adaptations**

Books can be licensed into other languages, regions, or even adapted into films, plays, or educational material.

- **Merchandise & Spin-Offs**
  Create products inspired by your book: journals, workbooks, coloring books, or branded merchandise.
  This extends your author brand while generating additional revenue.

- **Consulting & Coaching**
  If your book is nonfiction, it positions you as an expert.
  Offer one-on-one coaching, mentorship programs, or consulting packages.

Reflective Questions for Learners

- What opportunities beyond book sales could naturally align with your book's theme?
- Would you enjoy speaking, teaching, or coaching as part of your author journey?
- Can your book be adapted into different formats (e.g., audiobook, course, merchandise)?
- What "doors" do you want your book to open for you personally and professionally?

Activity: Your Expansion Map

Draw a circle in the center of a page labeled **"My Book."**

- Around it, write down **at least 5 possible opportunities** your book could lead to (e.g., speaking, merchandise, online course, consulting, adaptations).
- Circle the top 2 that excite you the most — these are your starting points for expansion.

Encouragement

Remember: **your book is not the end — it's the launchpad**. By thinking beyond sales, you transform from being "just an author" into **a creator, teacher, and entrepreneur**.

Your words can build platforms, communities, and even empires. Dream big.

Lesson 2: Repurposing Your Book

Your book is more than a finished product — it's a **content goldmine.** Repurposing allows you to transform your book into multiple formats, reaching new audiences and creating additional income streams.

Key Concepts

- **Audiobooks**
  >Audiobooks are one of the fastest-growing markets globally.
  >You can narrate your book yourself (for a personal touch) or hire a professional voice artist.
  >Platforms: Audible, ACX, Findaway Voices.

- **E-Courses & Workshops**
  >Break your book into modules and turn it into a structured online course or workshop.
  >Include slides, videos, worksheets, and interactive exercises.

- Workbooks & Companion Guides
  >If your book is nonfiction, create a workbook with exercises, prompts, and checklists.
  >Great upsell for readers who want to apply your lessons practically.

- **Blogs, Podcasts & Social Media** Content
  >Every chapter can become a blog post, podcast episode, or social media series.
  >Repurposing keeps your book alive in conversations long after launch.

- **Translations**
  >Translate your book into different languages to reach new markets (e.g., French, Swahili, Zulu).
  >Even partial translations (like summaries) can expand reach.

- **Adaptations**
  >Fiction books can inspire films, series, or plays.
  >Nonfiction books can become corporate training manuals or guides.

Reflective Questions for Learners

- Which format (audiobook, course, workbook, etc.) best suits your book's content?
- Do you prefer expanding through **digital products** (courses, audiobooks) or **physical companions** (workbooks, merchandise)?
- Who else could benefit from your book if it were repurposed differently (students, organizations, professionals)?
- What small repurposing step could you take this month to extend your book's life?

Activity: Repurposing Brainstorm

Take your book's **table of contents.**

- For each chapter, list **at least one way** you could repurpose it (e.g., Chapter 1 → blog post, Chapter 2 → podcast episode, Chapter 3 → course module).
- Circle 2–3 ideas you can realistically begin with after publishing.

Encouragement

Repurposing ensures your book **is never a one-time event**. Instead, it becomes a **living resource** that keeps generating value and impact.

Your words are flexible — don't lock them into one format. The more ways you share your message, the more people you'll reach.

Lesson 3: Building an Author Business

A successful author is not just a writer — but also a **business owner**. Your book can be the foundation of a sustainable career if you treat it as part of a bigger system rather than a one-time project.

Key Concepts

- **The Author as Entrepreneur**
  >Your book = your product.
  >Your name/brand = your business.
  >Think beyond selling one book; think of building an author ecosystem.

- **Multiple Streams of Income**
  >Book sales (print, eBook, audiobook).
  >Speaking engagements, workshops, coaching.
  >Merchandise, spin-off products, licensing deals.
  >Courses and membership communities.

- **Author Branding**
  >Create a consistent brand identity (logo, colors, author photo, tagline).
  >Your website should act as your **digital home base**.
  >Use newsletters and social media to nurture your reader community.

- **Business Infrastructure**
  Treat your writing as a business:
  >Register a business (where applicable).
  >Keep financial records (royalties, expenses, taxes).
  >Use contracts for collaborations.
  >Tools: accounting apps, email marketing platforms, publishing dashboards.

- **Scaling Your Author Business**
  >One book can lead to a series, which builds loyal readers.
  >Expand from one niche into others over time.
  >Collaborate with other authors, businesses, or organizations to scale impact.

Reflective Questions for Learners

- Do you see yourself as an author **and** an entrepreneur?
- What other products or services could your book naturally lead to?
- Have you considered building an **email list or website** to anchor your author brand?
- What tools or systems could help you manage your writing career more professionally?

Activity: Draft Your Author Business Plan

Take a fresh page and create a **1-page Author Business Plan** with these sections:

- **Vision**: What do you want your author career to look like in 5 years?
- **Products/Services:** Besides your book, what else can you offer?
- **Audience:** Who is your core reader community?
- **Channels:** How will you reach them (social media, email, events)?
- **Revenue Streams:** Where will your money come from?

Encouragement

Your book is not just a story or guide — it's a **seed**. With care, structure, and strategy, it can grow into a sustainable career and even an empire.

Remember: You are not only writing a book. You are building a legacy, a brand, and a business.

Lesson 4: Intellectual Property & Protection

As an author, your book is not only your creation — it's your **intellectual property (IP).** Protecting your rights ensures that your hard work, ideas, and earnings are safe while allowing you to benefit fully from your work.

Key Concepts

- **What is Intellectual Property (IP)?**
  >IP = creations of the mind (books, stories, poems, cover designs, brand names, etc.).
  >As soon as you write your book, you automatically own the copyright.

- **Copyright Basics**
  >Copyright gives you the exclusive right to reproduce, distribute, and sell your work.
  >In South Africa, copyright is automatic when you create a work, but registering it adds legal strength.
  >Duration: For literary works, copyright usually lasts for the author's life + 50 years (varies by country).

- **ISBN & Legal Deposits**
  >ISBN (International Standard Book Number) helps track and distribute your book globally.

>In South Africa, an ISBN is obtained from the National Library and requires you to send **legal deposit** copies to libraries.

- **Trademarks & Branding**
  >If you build a strong author brand or book series, you may consider trademarking names, series titles, or logos.
  >Example: A fantasy series with a unique brand identity can be trademarked for protection.

- **Contracts & Licensing**
  >Be cautious when signing contracts with publishers, distributors, or platforms.
  >Licensing: You can license your book for adaptations (e.g., film, TV, foreign translations). Always keep track of **who owns what rights**.

- **Plagiarism & Piracy**
  >Risks: Others may copy or illegally distribute your work.
  >Solutions: Use copyright notices, register works, and monitor online platforms.

Reflective Questions for Learners

- Do you know the copyright rules that apply in your country?
- Have you applied for an ISBN for your book?
- Are there elements of your author brand (logo, series name, pen name) that may need trademarking?
- Would you be comfortable licensing your book for other uses, or do you want to keep full control?

Activity: Protect Your Book

- Write a **Copyright Statement** for your book (include year, your name, and "All rights reserved").
- If you are in South Africa:
  >Research the National Library ISBN application process.
  >Write down the steps you'll take to get an ISBN.
- Create a list of rights you are willing to license (e.g., audiobook, translation) and those you want to keep.

Encouragement

Your words are valuable — and so are your rights. Protecting your intellectual property is like putting a lock on your creative house: it keeps you safe while giving you freedom to share confidently.

Owning and protecting your IP means you don't just write stories — you own assets. And assets build legacies.

Lesson 5: Long-Term Growth

Self-publishing is not just about one book — it's about building a career and a sustainable author brand. Long-term growth means creating systems, habits, and opportunities that allow you to keep writing, publishing, and expanding your reach year after year.

This lesson will guide you through strategies for staying relevant, scaling your author career, and ensuring your success compounds over time.

1. Focus on Consistent Output

- **Keep writing:** The best way to grow as an author is to publish more books — each new release expands your backlist and increases your visibility.
- **Series & connected works:** Readers love continuity. Writing series or related books keeps audiences engaged and loyal.
- **Experimentation:** Try different genres, formats (novellas, short stories), or collaborative works to reach new readers.

2. Build a Backlist Strategy

- **Backlist value:** Older books continue to generate income and bring in new readers.
- **Refresh & repackage**: Update covers, blurbs, or formatting to keep older titles competitive.
- **Box sets & bundles:** Combine books into collections for added value and higher royalties.

3. Invest in Your Author Platform

- **Website:** Keep it updated with your latest books, links, and news.
- **Email list:** Stay connected with readers through regular updates, sneak peeks, and exclusive content.

- **Social media presence:** Choose platforms where your target readers spend time and engage authentically.

4. Diversify Income Streams

Beyond royalties, consider:

- Paid speaking engagements.
- Online courses or workshops.
- Consulting for aspiring authors.
- Licensing deals for adaptations or translations.

5. Keep Learning & Adapting

- **Industry awareness:** Stay up to date with publishing trends, new platforms, and marketing tools.
- **Professional development:** Attend writer conferences, join author associations, or take advanced courses.
- **Adaptation**: Be ready to pivot your strategy as the market shifts (e.g., rise of audiobooks, AI tools, new distribution models).

6. Nurture Reader Relationships

- Treat your readers as a community, not just customers.
- Offer bonus content, Q&A sessions, or early access to new releases.
- Encourage reviews and testimonials — they drive long-term visibility.

Key Takeaways

Long-term growth comes from consistent output, building a strong backlist, and nurturing your author brand.

A sustainable career requires diversifying income, investing in your platform, and staying adaptable to industry changes.

Loyal readers are the foundation of growth — keep them engaged, valued, and part of your journey.

End-of-Module 6 Wrap-Up

Monetization & Long-Term Strategy

Congratulations! You've completed **Module 6: Monetization & Long-Term Strategy.** This module has taken you beyond the initial steps of writing and publishing, helping you think like a long-term, growth-oriented authorpreneur.

Here's a quick recap of what you've learned:

Key Lessons from Module 6:

1. Beyond Book Sales – How to expand your income streams with speaking, courses, consulting, and licensing opportunities.

2. Repurposing Your Book – Turning your book into multiple products (audiobooks, workbooks, blogs, online programs, etc.) for maximum reach and revenue.

3. Building an Author Business – Treating your writing career like a real business by setting systems, branding, and goals.

4. Intellectual Property & Protection – Safeguarding your creative work through copyright, ISBNs, and legal protections.

5. Long-Term Growth – Staying relevant through consistent publishing, building a backlist, nurturing readers, and adapting to industry changes.

Big Picture Takeaway

Self-publishing is more than just producing a book — it's building a sustainable career. With the right mindset, business strategy, and reader-first approach, you can keep growing long after your first launch.

This module has given you the blueprint to:

- Scale your author career.
- Diversify your income.
- Protect your work.
- Create lasting impact with your writing.

BONUS MODULE: The Future of Publishing & Emerging Opportunities

Learning Outcomes

By the end of this module, learners will:

- Stay ahead of trends shaping the publishing industry.
- Learn how to adapt their author strategies to new technologies.
- Explore unconventional but lucrative publishing avenues.
- Future-proof their self-publishing journey.

Lesson 1: The Rise of Digital-First Publishing

Why This Lesson Matters

Publishing is changing faster than ever. While traditional print books remain important, **digital-first publishing** has opened new doors for authors around the world. This lesson explores how focusing on digital formats first — eBooks, audiobooks, and online-first releases — can accelerate your publishing success, cut costs, and expand your reach globally.

What is Digital-First Publishing?

Digital-first publishing means **releasing your book in digital formats before (or sometimes instead of) print.** It prioritizes accessibility, speed, and adaptability in today's fast-moving book market.

Key Advantages of Digital-First Publishing

- **Global Reach** – Your book can instantly be available worldwide via Amazon Kindle, Apple Books, Kobo, and more.

- **Lower Upfront Costs** – Skip the expenses of print runs, warehousing, and physical distribution.
- **Faster Time-to-Market** – You can launch your book in weeks, not months.
- **Reader Accessibility** – Readers can download and start reading immediately.
- **Flexibility for Updates** – You can edit, update, or rebrand your book much more easily than with print.

Trends Driving Digital-First Publishing

- **eBook Popularity**: Millions of readers worldwide prefer digital convenience.
- **Audiobook Boom**: Audiobooks are one of the fastest-growing segments of publishing.
- **Mobile Reading**: Phones and tablets make it easier than ever for readers to engage with digital content.
- **Subscription Models**: Platforms like Kindle Unlimited are changing how people access books.

Potential Challenges

- **Digital Overcrowding**: The market is competitive — discoverability is key.
- **Piracy Risks**: Digital works can be copied, making protection important.
- **Reader Preferences**: Some readers still strongly prefer print books.

Practical Tips for Authors Going Digital-First

- Start with **professional eBook formatting** for smooth reader experiences.
- Consider releasing in **multiple digital formats** (ePub, PDF, Mobi, audiobook).
- Use **keywords and metadata** wisely to boost discoverability.
- Leverage **pre-orders** on digital platforms to build anticipation.
- Bundle your digital book with extras (checklists, worksheets, videos) to add value.

Activity: Digital First Exploration

- Research 2–3 **digital-first authors** in your genre.
- Note what strategies they use (pricing, design, promotions).
- Ask yourself: Could my next book benefit from a digital-first approach?

Lesson 2: Audiobooks & Voice Technology

Why This Lesson Matters

The way people consume books is evolving. Today's readers don'.t always have time to sit down with a print or digital book — but they do listen while commuting, exercising, cooking, or relaxing. **Audiobooks and voice technology** are now among the fastest-growing areas in publishing, offering self-published authors powerful new opportunities.

The Audiobook Boom

- **Explosive Growth**: Global audiobook sales are growing every year, with millions of new listeners.
- **Mainstream Platforms**: Audible, Google Play Books, Apple Books, and Spotify make distribution easier than ever.
- **Worldwide Reach**: Audiobooks can bring your work to global audiences, even in markets where print sales are limited.

Why Audiobooks Matter for Indie Authors

- **Accessibility** – Reach readers who prefer listening or who have visual impairments.
- **Multi-Tasking Readers** – Cater to busy audiences who consume books on the go.
- **Increased Earnings** – Diversify your income streams with another format.
- **Cross-Promotion** – Promote your audiobook alongside your eBook and print editions.
- **Long-Term Trend** – Voice-driven content consumption is here to stay.

Voice Technology in Publishing

Beyond audiobooks, **voice technology** is transforming storytelling and learning:

- **Smart Speakers** (Alexa, Google Home, Siri) – Readers can access your content hands-free.
- **Interactive Storytelling** – AI-driven voice tech allows readers to talk back to stories.
- **Podcasting Integration** – Authors can adapt books into serialized audio shows.

- **Language Accessibility** – Text-to-speech tools make your book available in multiple languages.

Challenges to Consider

- **Production Costs** – Professional narration can be expensive (but worth the quality).
- **Rights Management** – Ensure you retain control of your audiobook rights.
- **Marketing Efforts** – Audiobooks still require strong promotion to stand out.

Practical Tips for Authors

- Start with your **best-performing book** when testing audiobooks.
- Choose between **DIY narration** (if you have the voice skills) or **professional narrators**.
- Explore ACX (**Audiobook Creation Exchange**) or **Findaway Voices** for affordable production.
- Optimize your audiobook **metadata and keywords** just like you would for eBooks.
- Consider **bundling eBook + audiobook** for added reader value.

Activity: Audiobook Exploration

- Listen to 2–3 audiobooks in your genre.
- Pay attention to narration style, pacing, and quality.
- Ask yourself: Would my book work well as an audiobook? If yes, which chapters or scenes would shine in audio format?

You've now discovered the power of **audiobooks and voice technology**. This is not just a trend — it's a **new frontier** for authors who want to reach modern audiences.

Lesson 3: Global Publishing & Translation

Why This Lesson Matters

The publishing world is no longer confined to local markets. Thanks to digital platforms, authors can now reach readers across continents. However, language can be both a **barrier** and an

opportunity. Exploring **global publishing and translation** allows indie authors to tap into massive audiences, expand their brand internationally, and make their stories more inclusive.

The Global Market Opportunity

- **Millions of Readers Worldwide** – Most of the world's readers are not reading in English.
- **Digital Expansion** – Platforms like Amazon Kindle, Kobo, and Google Play make books instantly accessible worldwide.
- **Growing Demand for Diverse Voices** – Readers are hungry for authentic stories from Africa, Asia, Latin America, and beyond.
- **Revenue Potential** – Translated works often enjoy a second wave of sales in new markets.

Benefits of Translation for Authors

- **Reach Non-English Readers** – Open your work to audiences who prefer books in their native language.
- **Cultural Impact** – Share your story with different communities, building a stronger global brand.
- **Long-Term Royalties** – Translation can extend the life of your book, creating multiple income streams.
- **Discoverability** – In smaller language markets, your book may stand out more.
- **Adaptability** – Translations also open doors for **film, TV, and global collaborations.**

Challenges of Translation

- **Costs** – Professional translation can be expensive.
- **Accuracy** – A poor translation risks losing the spirit of your writing.
- **Cultural Nuances** – Direct translation may not always capture local idioms, humor, or context.
- **Marketing in New Regions** – Requires tailored strategies (different keywords, platforms, and reader habits).

How to Approach Global Publishing

- **Start Small** – Choose one or two markets (e.g., Spanish, French, or local African languages).
- **Hire Professionals** – Work with translators who understand both language and culture.

- **Use Translation Platforms** – Reedsy, Babelcube, and Upwork connect authors with translators.
- **Experiment with AI Tools** – Tools like DeepL or ChatGPT-assisted translation can support, but always use human editing.
- **Leverage Global Distributors** – Amazon, Smashwords, and Draft2Digital distribute to multiple countries.
- **Focus on Niche Communities** – For example, self-publishing in South African languages (Zulu, Xhosa, Afrikaans) can help you stand out.

Future Trends in Translation & Publishing

- **AI-Powered Translation** – Faster and cheaper but still requires human editing.
- **Multilingual eBooks** – Readers can switch between languages in a single edition.
- **Translated Audiobooks** – Expanding voice technology allows multi-language narration.
- **Cultural Partnerships** – Collaborating with international publishers for hybrid releases.

Activity: Global Thinking Exercise

- Imagine your book being read in another country. Which one excites you most?
- Write down 3 languages you'd like your book to be translated into — and why.
- Research whether your genre has demand in those regions (example: Romance in Brazil, Crime in Scandinavia, Inspirational Non-Fiction in Africa).

By embracing **global publishing and translation**, you open your author journey to the world stage. Your words can cross borders, cultures, and languages — ensuring your stories live far beyond where they were written.

Lesson 4: Community-Driven Publishing

Why This Lesson Matters

Publishing is no longer a one-way street where an author writes and readers passively consume. Today, communities of readers, writers, and supporters can actively shape the success of a book.

Community-driven publishing empowers authors to create with their audience, build loyal supporters, and even fund projects before a single page is printed.

What is Community-Driven Publishing?

It's an approach where **the power of readers, fans, and supporters directly influences the publishing process.** Instead of working alone, authors collaborate with their audience for:

- Feedback on ideas and drafts.
- Financial support (crowdfunding).
- Shared marketing and word-of-mouth.
- Long-term brand loyalty.

Examples of Community-Driven Models

- **Crowdfunding Platforms** – Sites like Kickstarter, Indiegogo, and GoFundMe allow authors to raise money upfront for editing, design, and printing.
- **Patronage Models** – Platforms like Patreon let fans subscribe monthly to support authors and receive exclusive content.
- **Beta Reader Groups** – Communities that give early feedback, improving story quality before publication.
- **Co-Creation** – Some authors invite readers to vote on character names, endings, or cover designs.
- **Collective Publishing Houses** – Groups of indie authors pooling resources for shared promotion and distribution.

Benefits of Community-Driven Publishing

- **Financial Support** – Reduce the burden of self-funding your project.
- **Built-In Audience** – Your supporters are your first readers and promoters.
- **Creative Feedback** – Gain valuable insights before launching.
- **Loyalty & Trust** – Readers feel invested in your journey.
- **Sustainability** – Repeat supporters can fund future books.

Challenges of This Approach

- **Time-Consuming** – Managing communities requires consistent engagement.
- **Unpredictability** – Crowdfunding success is not guaranteed.

- **Pressure** – Readers' involvement may limit creative freedom.
- **Platform Fees** – Some sites take a percentage of funds raised.

Practical Tips for Authors

- Start by **building your platform early** (social media, email lists, author websites).
- Offer **rewards or perks** to supporters (signed copies, exclusive chapters, live Q&As).
- Be transparent about **funding goals and project timelines.**
- Engage authentically — don't just sell; build relationships.
- Balance community input with your **creative vision.**

Activity: Community Vision Plan

- Write down 3 ways you could involve your readers in your next project.
- Explore one platform (Kickstarter, Patreon, or even a private Facebook group).
- Ask yourself: What would I offer my supporters in exchange for their trust and backing?

With community-driven publishing, you transform your audience from passive readers into active partners in your journey. This not only funds your book but builds a movement around your words.

Lesson 5: Future-Proofing Your Author Career

Why This Lesson Matters

The publishing landscape is constantly evolving — from the rise of eBooks to audiobooks, AI tools, and global readership. To thrive long-term, authors must think beyond just publishing their first book. **Future-proofing your author career** means preparing for shifts in technology, markets, and reader behavior, while building a foundation that sustains your writing journey for years to come.

The Core Principles of Future-Proofing

- **Adaptability** – Stay open to new formats (digital-first, audiobooks, interactive media).
- **Diversification** – Don't rely on one book; build multiple income streams.

- **Continuous Learning** – Keep up with publishing trends, marketing strategies, and new tools.
- **Strong Author Brand** – Readers will follow you across genres, platforms, and formats.
- **Community Building** – A loyal readership ensures longevity, no matter the industry changes.

Key Strategies for Authors

- **Expand Your Catalog** – The more books you publish, the more visibility and income streams you create.
- **Invest in Skills** – Learn marketing, design basics, or storytelling across media.
- **Leverage Technology** – Use AI tools for editing, translations, and audiobook production — but always add the human touch.
- **Go Global** – Consider translation, international distribution, and cross-border partnerships.
- **Create Evergreen Content** – Books that stay relevant (self-help, reference, children's books) generate long-term sales.
- **Think Beyond Books** – Monetize through speaking, teaching, consulting, or merchandise.

Future Trends to Watch

- **AI Storytelling Tools** – Helping authors brainstorm, edit, and even co-create.
- **Immersive Experiences** – AR/VR books, interactive storytelling, gamified literature.
- **Voice-First Publishing** – Audiobooks, podcasts, and smart-speaker integrations.
- **Blockchain & NFTs** – New ways of protecting rights and selling unique digital editions.
- **Global South Publishing Growth** – Africa, Asia, and Latin America are rising as major literary markets.

Potential Challenges

- Overdependence on one platform (e.g., only publishing on Amazon).
- Rapid tech changes leaving some books outdated.
- Burnout if you treat writing as a sprint, not a marathon.

Practical Tips for Staying Future-Proof

- Build a **personal website** as your permanent online home.
- Collect **email subscribers** — platforms may change, but your list is yours.

- Schedule time for **trend-watching** (follow publishing blogs, podcasts, industry reports).
- Network with other authors — communities adapt faster together.
- Always have a long-term vision: Where do you want to be in 5–10 years as an author?

Activity: Future Author Roadmap

- Write down **3 future-proof strategies** you can start implementing today (e.g., email list, multiple formats, learning marketing).
- Create a simple **5-year vision statement** for your author career.
- Identify one **new skill** (like audiobook production or translation research) to learn this year.

With **Future-Proofing**, you're not just writing books — you're building a **sustainable, adaptable, and thriving author career** that will stand strong no matter how the publishing industry evolves.

End-of-Module Wrap-Up

Congratulations! You've reached the end of this forward-looking module. By now, you've explored how the publishing industry is evolving and how **you can stay ahead of the curve** as an indie author.

What You've Learned in This Module

- **Digital-First Publishing**: Speed, affordability, and global reach.
- **Audiobooks & Voice Technology**: One of the fastest-growing markets in publishing.
- **Global Publishing & Translation**: Opening your work to worldwide audiences.
- **Community-Driven Publishing**: Turning readers into supporters, funders, and promoters.
- **Future-Proofing Your Career**: Building adaptability, resilience, and long-term strategies.

Reflection Questions

Take a moment to think about your own author journey:

- Which **future publishing opportunity** excites you the most?
- Could you imagine your book being translated or turned into an audiobook?
- How can you start building a **future-proof author plan** today?

Encouragement

The publishing world is no longer limited by gatekeepers or geography. **You hold the power** to shape your destiny as an author. Whether through digital-first publishing, community-driven support, or exploring new technologies, the opportunities are endless.

Think of this toolkit not just as a guide for publishing your first book, but as your **companion for a lifetime of writing and growth**.

Remember: Your words have the power to outlast trends, borders, and even time itself.

You've now completed the **Self-Publishing Mastery Toolkit** — a step-by-step manual designed to help you write, publish, and promote your book with confidence.

Final Wrap-Up: Your Journey as an Author Begins Now

Congratulations! You've reached the end of the Self-Publishing Mastery Toolkit. By completing this guide, you've taken a bold step into the exciting and empowering world of self-publishing.

This is more than just a book — it is your **manual, your compass, and your reliable companion** on the road to becoming a successful author.

What You've Achieved

Throughout this journey, you've discovered how to:

- Turn your ideas into structured, publishable books.
- Edit and polish your manuscript to professional standards.
- Format and design books that readers love to hold and read.
- Publish confidently across major platforms.
- Market and build an audience that grows with you.
- Monetize your work and plan for long-term growth.
- Explore the future of publishing — from audiobooks to global translations.

You've gained not just knowledge, but also **practical tools, activities, and strategies** to make your dream of becoming a published author a reality.

Your Next Step

The real journey begins now. Books are not written, published, and forgotten. They live, breathe, and travel — carrying your voice, your vision, and your story to places you may never go physically.

Take the outline, plan, and strategies you've built here, and put them into action:

- Choose your book idea.
- Set your writing schedule.
- Commit to publishing — your voice matters.

A Personal Note to You

Every author starts where you are right now — with a dream, a blank page, and the courage to take the first step. Your story matters. Your words have the power to heal, to inspire, to educate, and to entertain.

Think of this toolkit as your **pilot's manual**. Just as a pilot relies on instruments to navigate the skies, you now have the **tools to navigate publishing**. With persistence, passion, and the right mindset, your book can truly take flight — and even become a bestseller.

Final Encouragement

This is your moment.

The world is waiting for your stories, your knowledge, and your voice. Don't let doubt or fear hold you back. You are ready.

Go ahead, write the book, publish it, and share it with the world. You are now officially an author — and this is only the beginning of your journey.

www.ingramcontent.com/pod-product-compliance
Lightning Source LLC
Chambersburg PA
CBHW081017040426
42444CB00014B/3252